a year in the life of westonbirt sarah howard

F

FRANCES LINCOLN LIMITED

PUBLISHERS

a year in the life of
westonbirt
sarah howard

words by gail mckenzie
foreword by colin tudge

For my Mum and Dad who first
brought me to Westonbirt, and
throughout my childhood instilled
in me a deep appreciation of our
landscape and natural world.

Frances Lincoln Limited
4 Torriano Mews
Torriano Avenue
London NW5 2RZ
www.franceslincoln.com

A Year in the Life of Westonbirt
Copyright © Frances Lincoln Limited 2009

Photographs copyright © Sarah Howard 2009
Words copyright © Gail McKenzie 2009
Foreword copyright © Colin Tudge 2009

First Frances Lincoln edition 2009

A catalogue record for this book is available from the British Library

ISBN 978-0-7112-3025-5

Printed in Singapore

9 8 7 6 5 4 3 2

HALF TITLE *Acer palmatum*
TITLE PAGE Winter light

contents

foreword
colin tudge

We human beings could reasonably build our entire lives around trees. In fact, that would be one of the most reasonable things we could do.

Everything about them is impressive. There are bristlecone pines on the hills of California that are more than 5,000 years old – as old as the craft of writing and as old, therefore, as written history. They were already ancient when Moses led the Israelites out of Egypt. Closer to home there are yews in Britain that pre-date John the Baptist. Some trees are huge – the biggest of all living creatures: some of the Coastal Redwoods of California are almost twice the height of the leaning tower of Pisa, and there's a banyan in India that covers two thirds of an acre.

In reality, trees seem to do all the things that they are said to do in the world's great mythology. They do indeed mediate between earth and sky; they partake of both in equal measure. Aristotle said that everything in the world is compounded from earth, air, fire and water – and with trees this is obviously the case. They build their great trunks and branches mainly from air – from the carbon in carbon dioxide. They join the carbon dioxide with hydrogen extracted from water, to form carbohydrate. They combine carbohydrate with nitrogen and other minerals drawn from the earth. They power this whole process by photosynthesis – tapping in to the energy of the sun; and although the sun is a very peculiar kind of fire, a fire it very definitely is.

As they do all these things, trees make the world a very agreeable place to be. By drawing up water from the soil and releasing it from their leaves they regulate the rainfall. South America would be a dry and barren place indeed were it not for the trees of Amazonia, creating the rainclouds. By drawing in carbon dioxide by the million ton the world's forests stop the world from over-heating; indeed, we could do more to curb global warming by looking after ancient forests than by any other means that are open to us. All over the world trees create the microclimates, the green shade, that human beings – and other animals –

favour above all. As if all this was not enough they also provide us with the world's most versatile and forgiving material for building; with paper; with the world's most renewable fuel; with a host of foods; and, for good measure, with a seemingly endless list of fibres and gums and pigments and medicines and oils and unguents. We could easily build our entire agriculture around trees – and there is a good case for doing so. Indeed, it would make perfect sense to build our entire economy, our whole life-strategy, around them. Absolutely not should we take them for granted. If we care about ourselves, and our children and our children's children, then we should look after the trees.

But we won't look after trees, or any other wild creature, or indeed our own kind, unless we give a damn. That is the absolute requirement. And this, more than anything else, is what gardens are for – places like the magnificent arboretum of Westonbirt. They help us to appreciate. You can learn from Westonbirt's trees, of course – it's a great place to study botany and social history – but the main thing to take from them is simply how wonderful they are. The appropriate emotion is not awe, although some of them are awesome enough. It is reverence, and gratitude, that creatures like this should exist at all. Once we realize these things – how wonderful trees are, and how much we owe to them – then we have a far better chance of putting the whole world to rights. If we don't take good care of the world's trees, we have very little chance indeed.

All in all, then, I am delighted to be given this opportunity to introduce this wonderful celebration of Westonbirt. Sarah took these photographs in all seasons at all times of day, reflecting the essential ambivalence of trees; on the one hand their monumentality; and on the other, that they are living creatures, always active, constantly adjusting. In this the book, truly, is a mirror held up to nature.

Colin Tudge is the author of *The Secret Life of Trees* (Penguin, 2006).

a photographer's eye
sarah howard

I first visited Westonbirt Arboretum as a child with my parents. It was autumn, the leaves were falling and the trees shone with their bright display. I recall having a wonderful time laughing and running through this vast world of colour, among the piles of rustling leaves. It was magical then and, years later, the magic remains.

In 2007 I revisited Westonbirt – again in autumn. This time, seeing it through a photographer's eye, it left even more of an impression. It was then that I decided to create a book, a celebration of the arboretum, focusing on the beauty and magnificence of this incredible collection – among which are some of the world's oldest and rarest trees and shrubs.

To record the changing seasons was perhaps the most obvious way of doing this, so over the next 15 months I returned to Westonbirt many times, capturing each season in turn with the aim of creating images that were more than just record shots, images that really captured the essence of the arboretum.

Summer perhaps proved to be the most testing of all the seasons with its all-encompassing shades of green and harsh light. I found myself turning to the wonderful barks with their textures and colours, the shape of various leaves, and also to the early mornings when the light shone through the foliage, its rays penetrating deep into the woodland.

I have to confess that I am slightly obsessed by trees – they never cease to leave me with a sense of wonder. Whether it's their vast size, age, complexity, or the very fact they change colour, lose their leaves, and then a few months later spring forth delicate sticky buds and the cycle begins all over again. With some of the older specimens that have far outlived many humans of their time, I cannot help but reflect on what they have witnessed in their lifetime.

I feel I know the arboretum well now, and I do of course have my special places and indeed favourite trees. One such place is Lime Avenue in the Old Arboretum, which in early summer is truly beautiful: a vast tunnel of tranquil green. There is also an incredibly characterful birch tree on Mitchell Drive that always grabs my attention, its huge branches stretching out, and the fabulous texture of the peeling bark.

Whatever the season it always leaves an impression. I call it 'Magnificence' – a title I find very fitting. It is otherwise known as *Betula ermanii* or Erman's birch.

I recall on one autumnal visit, a stunning Japanese maple completely stopped me in my tracks. It stood in a slight clearing and shone so incredibly brilliantly, taking centre stage among all the other brightly coloured acers. For me she was the 'Star of the Show'.

Autumn cries out to photographers and so they come, all drawn to the vibrant display of foliage, shutters clicking as they each try to take away a little bit of Westonbirt.

In winter, the arboretum is suddenly devoid of colour, leaves gone, trees left stark and naked. With the days often dull I focused on capturing the early morning rays of light, the long shadows and then of course, when it came, the wonderful frost. With its arrival suddenly Westonbirt is transformed into a winter wonderland. Canopies of white with leaves held still in time, branches peering through the mist. And where there are no leaves, a frosty dusting of silvery white creates a temporary display. I was also lucky enough to witness snow and just for a few brief hours, the arboretum is carpeted in white, and again, a transformation occurs. Everything is suddenly very still and it looks and feels truly magical. All too soon it was gone.

I hope that through my images I have done Westonbirt Arboretum justice. Of course one could spend longer, as with any subject, but this is not designed to be a definitive record of all that the arboretum holds, more a showcase of some of the shining stars and special places that are to be found in this wonderful collection.

My equipment:
Fuji S5 Pro digital camera
Lenses: Sigma 12–24mm, Nikon 28–105mm
and 70–300mm
Lee filters
Manfrotto tripod

All the images in this book may be purchased as fine art prints. Sarah also offers one-to-one photography tutorials. Please visit: www.sarahhowardphotography.com

a garden for all seasons

a garden for all seasons

A garden for all seasons – welcoming in the spring with blousy magnolias and blushing rhododendrons, drifting into the vibrant greens of summer and reaching a fiery crescendo in autumn. And as the year turns, Westonbirt becomes a serene and magical place in which to find some solitude and contemplate what lies ahead.

But two hundred years ago, Westonbirt Arboretum was just open fields lazily nibbled by sheep. And at that time a man of great vision took this 'blank canvas' and started to transform 600 acres of Gloucestershire land into one of the greatest tree gardens in the world.

The man in question was one Robert Holford – a gentleman of great means and, in true Victorian style, an enthusiastic and indulgent collector – passionate about plants, but also blessed with an artist's eye. With wealth came leisure, and the Holford family clearly relished the early days of these pleasure grounds, trotting down the rides in horse-drawn carriages, and ambling along curvaceous paths. But ultimately what Robert Holford was doing was leaving a growing legacy for future generations to enjoy.

Today, Westonbirt is an internationally important arboretum with over 16,000 trees and shrubs, from much-loved natives to rare exotics from as far afield as Japan and Australia. And here reside many champion trees – some of the biggest, tallest and rarest in the world.

From the beginning, Holford imbued Westonbirt with its spirit, and ever since the caretakers of this land have safeguarded its soul – right up to today, when it is in the care of the Forestry Commission. Now, this private passion can be shared by many thousands of people throughout the changing seasons.

A wealth of plants

Robert Holford's grand plan was to create not only a beautiful landscape but also the best collection of trees in the country. Fortunately for him, he came from a wealthy family. Four generations had been leading judges in London and his father was head of the New River Company, which brought fresh water to London from aquifers under the Westonbirt estate.

Given his artistic bent, Holford was heavily influenced by the earlier ideas of William Sawrey Gilpin. Gilpin was an artist turned landscape advisor and a leading exponent of the 'Picturesque' style. He had applied the principles of painting to enhance the landscape, and at Westonbirt trees were planted together as much for their aesthetic charm as for any scientific correctness.

In his time Gilpin had toured the countryside, sketching as he went. He noted the masts of ships breaking the line of the shore, and trees breaking the extent of a lawn. And so it was to be at Westonbirt. Sculptured incense cedars and towering redwoods reach for the skies, textured and peeling barks create detail and around every corner comes a new scene. Everywhere you wander dark screens of evergreen yew, box and laurel act not only as windbreaks but also as subtle backdrops, showing off their ornamental neighbours to best effect.

Scouring the globe

Robert Holford could have whatever plant he wanted – so long as it would survive in this temperate climate, and that he could track it down. And this was the age of curiosity, and of the great plant hunters. There was hot competition between many of the landed gentry to collect the most exotic plants for their great estates, and they guarded these natural treasures jealously. Holford was, so to speak, 'at the top of his tree'.

Famous and intrepid plant hunters such as Scotsman David Douglas in North America and Cotswold-born Ernest Wilson in China, sent back unknown and exciting seeds for propagation. Today, these stand proud in the arboretum as Douglas firs (*Pseudotsuga menziesii*) and handkerchief trees (*Davidia involucrata*), among many other rare beauties. In North America, Douglas lived off the land, befriending local tribes and in just two years covering 6,000 miles of rough territory in his endless quest for new plants. Wilson was equally determined and talented. In one four-month period alone, it is thought that he introduced over 1,000 new species from China.

Planting began in earnest in the 1850s, starting at the eastern end of what is now the Old Arboretum. Holford thought he had inherited a largely chalky soil but to his delight he spotted rabbits and badgers furiously digging away and throwing up showers of sandy loam around the now glorious Savill Glade. He could have all the showy lime-hating, acid-loving rhododendrons, camellias and magnolias he so craved. From here on his skill and ambitions flourished, and from 1855 rides radiated out across the land, punctuated by quiet glades and paths. Soon the Holford family were residing in a stately house, now a school, affording sweeping vistas of their newly extended gardens.

A living legacy

Robert Holford's greatest artistic work was to be Acer Glade – in autumn the Japanese maples here are a riot of reds and golds. The Holfords chose to entertain guests royally in its 'Colour Circle', treating them to sumptuous picnics as they absorbed the autumnal sights and scents of maples, Persian ironwoods and the sweet candyfloss smell of Katsura trees.

Robert's son George followed in his footsteps. Together they cut swathes through the ancient, wilder Silk Wood, and honed their propagation skills – often in great secret. Trees arrived by train and cart, and soil supposedly from China.

And so Westonbirt blossomed – with a more formal air in the older part of the arboretum and a slightly more relaxed approach in Silk Wood. Here, the open and carefully managed woods and rides have become home to a whole host of wildlife – from badgers, bats and butterflies to wild flowers and fungi.

On George's death in 1926, the estate passed to his nephew Lord Morley. The mansion and grounds were sold off, but the arboretum flourished under the then curator W. J. Mitchell. But in 1956 it passed to the Crown in lieu of death duties, and thence to the Forestry Commission. In these safe and skilful hands, Westonbirt has become the world-famous and much-loved tree garden it now is – a place the Holfords would be rightly proud of.

the emergence of spring

spring

Camellia red, rhododendron pink, bluebell blue… an artist has picked up her palette and colour-washed the plants. In spring, Westonbirt is drenched in soft hues, and many would argue that this season is its best-kept secret.

As winter eases and days stretch out, welcome signs of new life emerge. In February, delicate hazel catkins dance on bare stems and wild honeysuckle dares to put on an early show. As March approaches, the first camellia buds unfurl and burst into rosy red, and the huge, hairy magnolia buds pop open. Flamboyant 'goblet' flowers on some of the Himalayan magnolias (*Magnolia campbellii*) reach the size of dinner plates.

Unlike acid-loving camellias, magnolias are less fussy about the soil in which they put down their roots, and happily blossom all over the arboretum. And alongside the showy blooms, there are more delicate 'star' magnolias (*Magnolia stellata*) with fragrant, white star-shaped flowers.

Soon these early spring players are joined and seemingly upstaged by the dazzling rhododendrons – an obvious favourite of George Holford, which thrive on acid soils around the Old Arboretum. Westonbirt's innumerable rhododendrons are the A-list celebrities of spring.

Many of these exotic plants are over 100 years old and as such great natural treasures – often introduced from China by renowned Victorian plant hunters, and now towering overhead in a dizzy cloud of colour. Another gem lies in a later-flowering magnolia sent back by the famous Gloucestershire plant hunter Ernest Wilson. He even lent his name to this particularly fine creamy magnolia (*Magnolia wilsonii*), with its crimson-centred flowers and heady scent.

By late April, the seasonal performance is in full swing – richly coloured rhododendrons and heavenly scented azaleas abound, and over in Silk Wood a small corner of the Far East has arrived. In a quiet glade, Japanese and Chinese flowering cherry trees (*Prunus*) are cloaked in pale pink blossom, showering petals in the gentlest of warm breezes. Nearby is Sargent's cherry (*Prunus sargentii*), often said to be the most beautiful of all the cherries, and an impressive old-timer that gently bows to passing visitors as they stroll along the path. This is the famous species that turns the slopes of Mount Fuji pink each spring.

In May, one Westonbirt beauty is a sure crowd pleaser. The impressive and aptly named handkerchief tree (*Davidia involucrata*) waves papery white flowering bracts from every branch. Even the autumn stars are putting in an interesting early appearance. As the Japanese maples (*Acer palmatum*) slowly unfurl their exquisite leaves they also demand attention.

On the wilder side, wood anemones, primroses and celandines give way to carpets of 'Monet' May bluebells – a sure sign of a well-managed ancient oak woodland, with clearings to let the light stream down on to the woodland floor, stirring the wildlife. Everywhere, the hazy shades of the bluebells contrast with the acid yellow of dandelions, also out to gain a little of the spring glory.

LEFT **Early morning dew on rhododendron**

RIGHT **Looking to the sky through magnolias**

TOP *Magnolia campbellii*
BOTTOM LEFT AND RIGHT
Rhododendron
BOTTOM CENTRE **Magnolia**

ABOVE LEFT *Magnolia sprengeri* x *campbellii*
ABOVE CENTRE AND RIGHT
Camellia petals and bud
RIGHT *Rhododendron decorum*

ABOVE **Spring blossom**
RIGHT **Magnolias flowering**

Spring flowers in Silk Wood

Betula ermanii on
Mitchell Drive

OPPOSITE Buttercups

FOLLOWING PAGE Bluebells
and blossoms

leafy glades of summer

Westonbirt has gone green. Strolling under the softly rustling summer canopy of Lime Avenue, all seems right with the world. Heavily scented yellow blossoms drip from the 'cathedral' arches of these largely common limes (*Tilia x europaea*), drawing in bees in their droves and sending them bumbling on their way after an overindulgence on nectar.

Only in summer do you sense the true size and scale of this tranquil tree garden. Shiny new leaves soak up the rays, flowers bloom and bees and butterflies take flight. Subdued green may be the predominant summer shade, but here and there are bold splashes of colour, such as the dangling waxy red flowers, quite fuchsia-like, of the lantern trees (*Crinodendron hookerianum*).

Not to be outdone by the springtime 'chandelier' flowers of our native horse chestnuts (*Aesculus hippocastanum*), Indian horse chestnuts (*Aesculus indica*) save their best for the summer flower show. And Westonbirt has some of the finest in the country. Around the longest day, these tall Himalayan trees conjure up a mass of orchid-like, white and

Platanus orientalis
(Oriental plane)

35

pink-sprayed blooms that stand out against the lush green backdrop. And in one final burst of glory, their leaves will turn to yellow and orange for autumn. Their timber has proved useful too. For almost two centuries it was made into packing cases for tea exported from India to Britain.

Tulips seem to have taken to the trees. High up in an American tulip tree (*Liriodendron tulipifera*) – one of the largest exotic trees ever introduced into Britain – sit yellow tulip-shaped flowers tinged with orange. Slightly less exotic, but equally charming, Waterer laburnums (*Laburnum x watereri*) are weighed down with golden cascades of flowers and hydrangeas wear heavy balls of cream and blue-tinted blooms.

For sheer size and style, the oriental plane can't be beaten. The magnificent, spreading canopy of this broad-leaved tree offers shade from the sun, and the tree itself has a distinguished past. It is one of the parents of the hybrid London plane, commonly planted as a street tree in cities. Not only does this offspring shade passers-by but like all planes it is also pretty tolerant of pollution – thanks to its patchwork of peeling bark and super-resistant glossy leaves.

Throughout the long summer, the smoke bushes (*Cotinus coggygria*) smoulder. Wispy purplish plumes create a smoke-like halo over each shrub, which slowly fades to a fine smoky grey. Related to pistachios and mangoes, these bushes grow naturally across southern Europe to the Himalayas.

Natural tree sculpture, Old Arboretum

Acer palmatum ssp. *amoenum* (Japanese maple)

It is along Holford Ride that Robert Holford engineered one of his finest vistas. From the family home at one end, the ride strikes out across the arboretum, taking in Lime Avenue to the right, and along the way planted informally yet cleverly with fine specimens, such as incense cedars (*Calocedrus decurrens),* full-moon maples (*Acer japonicum*), towering redwoods and Scots pines (*Pinus sylvestris*). Giant redwoods or wellingtonias (*Sequoiadendron giganteum*) first arrived as seeds in 1853 from their native Sierra Nevada in California. They are believed to be the largest living things on Earth – some weighing up to 2,000 tonnes and reaching 3,000 years old. And such was the hype around these monumental trees that Holford was willing to part with up to two guineas for a single seed.

Westonbirt deserves to be as famous for its native wild plants as it is for its cultivated ones. A Silk Wood summer notches up rare great butterfly orchids (*Platanthera chlorantha*) and meadow saffron (*Colchicum autumnale*), oaks and beeches. And with the flowers and trees come wild animals – speckled wood butterflies, rare bats and shuffling, snuffling badgers, and swallows swooping on insects over the Downs. It's a secret and secure place to frequent – for both wildlife and humans.

Birch trees, Silk Wood

Tree arch, Silk Wood

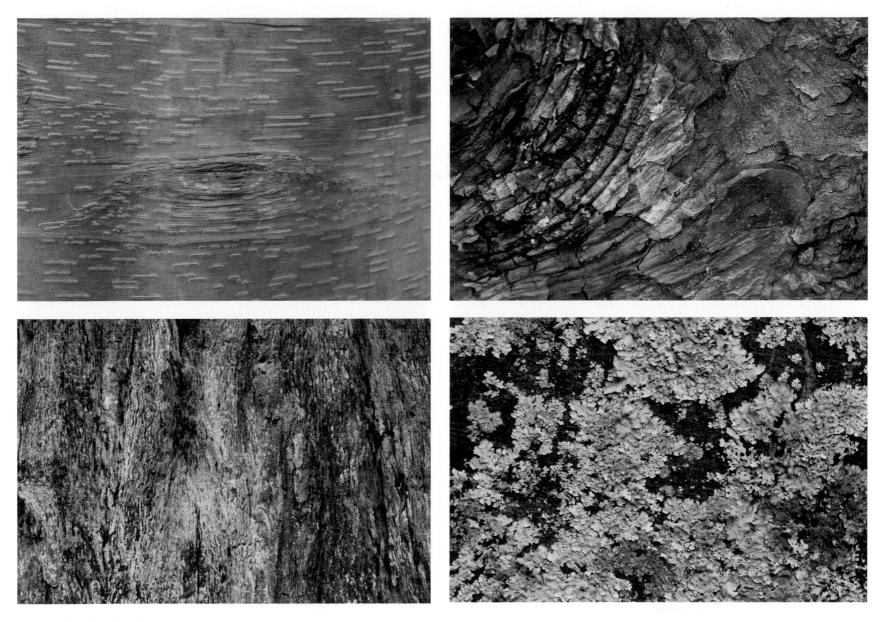

A tactile bark collection

The never-ending cycle of
seed to flower to seed is played
out week by week year on year,
here with the common dandelion

Acer palmatum

PREVIOUS PAGE Common
larch among grasses in
Silk Wood

OPPOSITE Fern in the breeze
BELOW Fern detail

THIS PAGE, TOP LEFT AND RIGHT
Conifer foliage and bud
MIDDLE LEFT *Cornus kousa*
MIDDLE RIGHT Seeds of rare
Dipteronia sinensis
BOTTOM LEFT *Acer
pectinatum*
BOTTOM RIGHT Dew on
smoke bush

Bracken beneath
hybrid larch
in Silk Wood

kaleidoscope of autumn colour

autumn

Days shorten, temperatures dip, and nature puts on one last performance – the very best it can muster. And Westonbirt boasts one of the finest – fiery reds Japanese maples (*Acer palmatum*), plum-purple Persian ironwoods (*Parrotia persica*) and the pure gold and copper of American hickories (*Carya*) and native beeches (*Fagus sylvatica*). Adults simply stand and stare; children run wild, clutching leaf and fir cone treasures.

At first the seasonal changes are subtle, masked by the persisting green. Come September, spindles (*Euonymus*) and full moon maples are beginning to turn, and as October progresses, red, orange and yellow rapidly coat the delicate leaves of Japanese maples. Westonbirt is home to the largest collection in Britain, and Acer Glade its famed autumn 'Mecca'. But shrewd annual 'leaf-peepers' are increasingly heading for the younger National Collection of Japanese maples in Silk Wood, where planting of 250 different cultivars started in the 1980s. In all, about 300 cultivated varieties create a dazzling Westonbirt display.

Not all the sensory delights of autumn can be seen. One you just smell coming…a sweet candyfloss scent pervading the air across the arboretum. As the heart-shaped leaves of the much-loved katsura tree (*Cercidiphyllum japonicum*) turn buttery yellow they proffer an intoxicating olfactory delight.

Another exotic gem from the Far East is the gingko or maidenhair tree (*Ginkgo biloba*), whose fan-shaped leaves go from fresh green to bright yellow to mark the changing season. This sacred 'fossil' tree was around at the time of the dinosaurs, 160 million years ago, and has somehow survived to this day. In Japan, it was one of the few plants to survive the Hiroshima atomic bomb, and is seen as a symbol of hope and prosperity.

By November many of these glamorous trees are beginning to shed their leaves, just as others are coming into their own and spreading the show right through the month. The needles of the deciduous dawn redwood (*Metasequoia glyptostroboides*) take on a beautiful tawny shade and the American hickories and oaks turn yellow and red. On a misty autumnal morning the native beeches are a sea of fluttering coppery leaves – hanging on until the very last.

Autumn is a harvest festival for both wildlife and humans. Jewel-like hips and berries adorn many trees and shrubs, and conkers dropping from the grand old horse chestnuts are hoarded hungrily.

'Will it be a spectacular autumn?' There's an endless debate about what weather conditions prompt the best show. For most species, warm summers followed by sunny days and cold crisp nights tend to bring out their best colours. But the sheer wealth and variety of the world's trees and shrubs at Westonbirt ensure that every year is a good year.

Each plant is set to its own native biological clock and as one star fades another creeps up behind it and refreshes the riot of colour. And all the while, as the leaves take their turn to colour and fall, so the woodland floor is afforded a soft multi-coloured carpet of red, yellow and gold – perfect for tramping through and gently kicking up with a well-worn boot.

Autumn is the crescendo of the four seasons – think of a colour and one of Westonbirt's trees will be displaying it somewhere. It never fails to lift the spirits.

Carpet of colour

Acer palmatum ssp.
matsumurae (Japanese
Maple)

Acer Glade

Betula ermanii, Mitchell Drive

Fagus sylvatica
(Common beech)

ABOVE AND RIGHT *Acer
palmatum* ssp. *amoenum*
(Japanese maple)

Morning rays

Acer palmatum ssp.
matsumurae (Japanese maple)

Betula ermanii,
Mitchell Drive

BELOW AND OPPOSITE PAGE BOTTOM
Maple leaves
OPPOSITE PAGE TOP Colour burst,
Old Arboretum

'Magnificence' (*Betula ermanii*),
Mitchell Drive

73

PREVIOUS PAGE CLOCKWISE
Liriodendron tulipifera
on Jackson Avenue,
Beeches on Loop Walk,
First rays

RIGHT *Platanus orientalis*
(Oriental plane)

Beech leaf panorama

Norway maple

'Star of the Show',
Acer palmatum

winter wonderland

winter

Life's simple pleasures – the crunch of frozen soil underfoot, hoar frost spiking every branch, brief sunshine glancing off glossy bark. Leaves have long gone and the true architecture of the Westonbirt landscape is laid bare, all quiet corridors and columns of trees.

As early morning mists lift, conifers and evergreens come into their own and present their best profiles: tall spires of Serbian spruce (*Picea omorika*), weighty limbs of cedar of Lebanon (*Cedrus libani*) and glorious golden Scots pine (*Pinus sylvestris* 'Aurea'). Against these dark outlines, holly berries and clumps of dogwood (*Cornus alba*) add a little seasonal red cheer. Why is the dogwood so called? Some suggest the name comes from the old English word for dagger 'dag', and certainly the wood was used for making skewers and daggers; others would have it that the name is based on its reported use in washing dogs!

Defying the bitter cold, yellow and red spider-like flowers decorate the leafless witch hazels (*Hamamelis*) and tiny crimson flowers dust the stems of Persian ironwoods. Slow-growing corkscrew hazel (*Corylus avellana* 'Contorta') is also at its best – extravagantly twisted stems dangling with long yellow catkins. This is a form of our native hazel – first discovered in a Gloucestershire hedgerow in the early 1860s.

For twelve enchanted nights at Christmas the trees take on a whole new, glittering appearance. Elaborately dressed in thousands of eco-friendly lights, their majestic forms are seen in a completely new light. Thousands of visitors of all ages ritually stroll through this magical scene to recapture the essence of the festive season.

Winter not only exposes the silhouettes of the magnificent trees but also brings to the fore many fine-textured barks. The Tibetan cherry (*Prunus serrula*) sports a smooth, mahogany cloak; Erman's birch (*Betula ermanii*) wears a shaggy creamy white coat; a Chinese paper-bark maple (*Acer griseum*) dramatically flakes off its rust-red outer skin and the snake-bark maple's stripy bark (*Acer davidii*) speaks for itself. All are just crying out to be touched.

Within this serene setting, birds are busying themselves among the trees – woodpeckers, tree creepers and flitting tits. The world never truly stands still. This is also a traditional time in which to carry out woodland work. In Silk Wood, the hazel 'understorey' is coppiced just as it was hundreds of years ago, and used to make hurdles and beanpoles.

Also on site, coppicers are cutting this amazing renewable resource to slow burn and blacken into charcoal. As hazel and oak are carefully removed so the ancient wood opens up and vigorous new growth can get underway, ensuring a new generation of trees for years to come. Birds and wild flowers prosper and beetles and bugs enjoy the housing benefits of dead and rotting trees, which have been left standing just as they were found.

Plants may even choose to flower in the long winter months. In February, Cornelian cherries (*Cornus mas*) break into flower, with huge numbers of small blooms decorating naked stems. Snowdrops push their nodding heads up out of the cold earth and even the camellia and rhododendron buds begin to swell.

Another magical year may be over at Westonbirt, but new signs of life are quick to put in an appearance and break the winter spell.

Through the mist

Winter's chill

Silhouettes

Beeches on The Downs

Betula ermanii,
Mitchell Drive

Canopy of frost

Weeping birch,
Betula pendula 'Youngii'

Lime Avenue
in winter

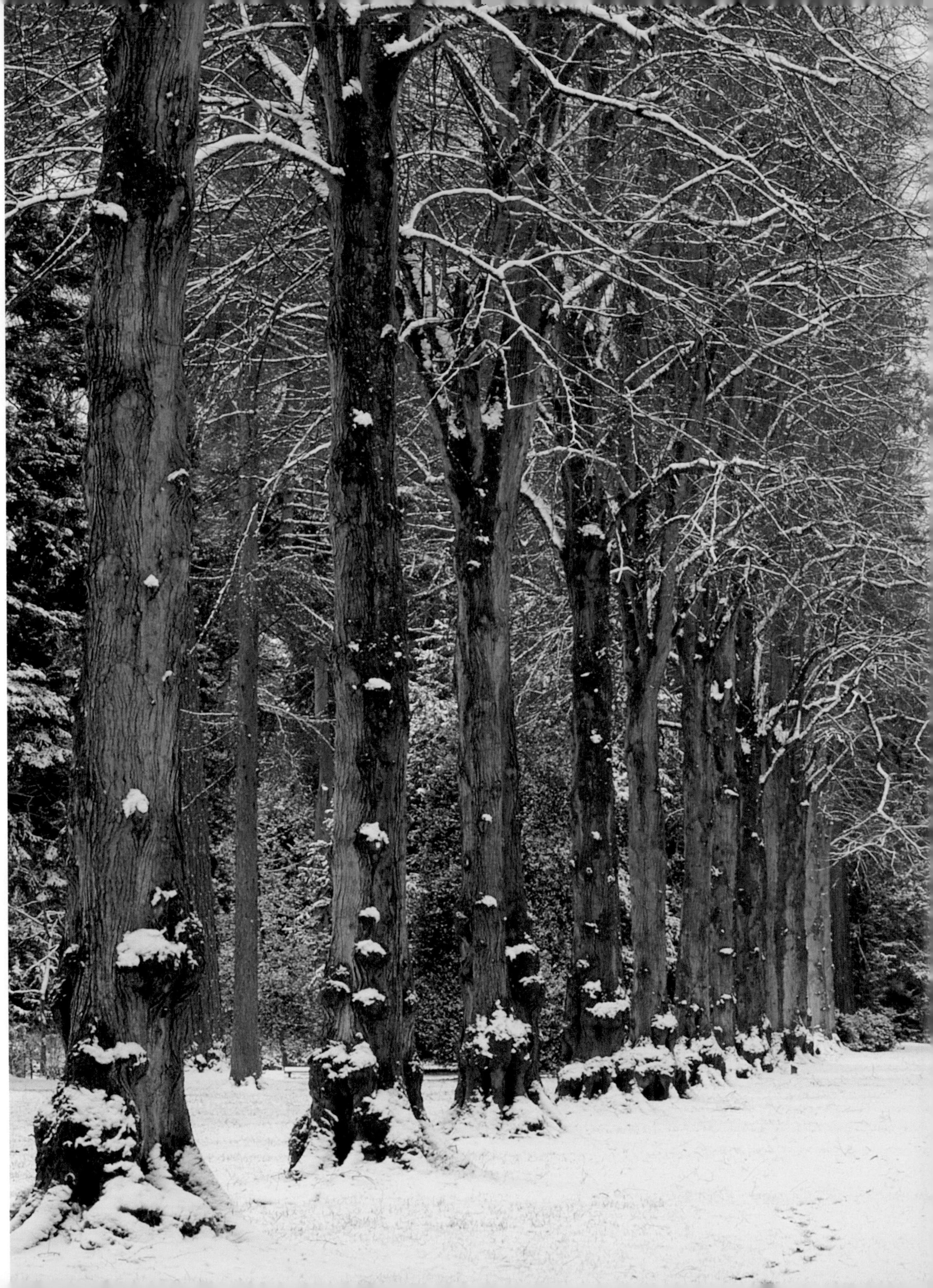

Stag-headed oak

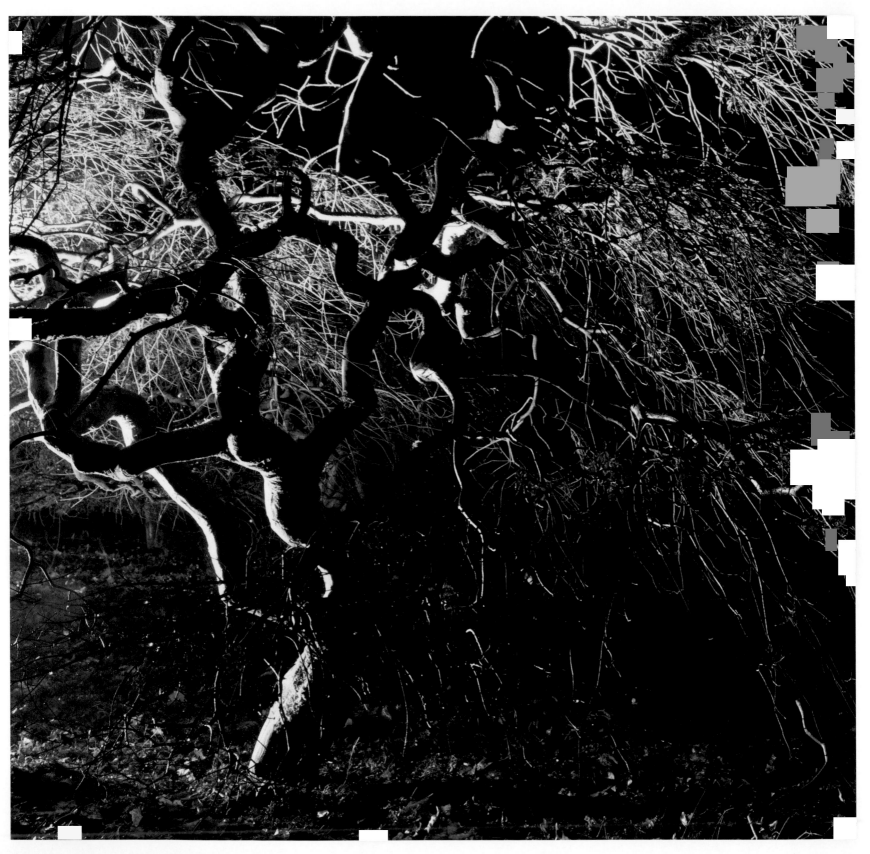

Enchanted Christmas –
Old Arboretum trees lit up
for a truly magical season

Mossy woodland glade

Winter shadows

gardening on a grand scale

Working at Westonbirt could be likened to working on the Forth Bridge. You set out with a plan at one end, work though meticulously, then go back to the beginning and start all over again. Trees need constant care and a 'picturesque' landscape such as Westonbirt's doesn't just happen.

Like any garden, as trees grow some become overcrowded while others are sadly struck down by disease or even storms. Wise planning is paramount – trees are slow to grow and any planted now will not mature for several decades. And to maintain the 'picturesque' landscape, overgrown glades and views must be kept clear and tidy.

Westonbirt is fortunate in having an extremely skilled team of arborists who carry out the bulk of the work, supported by keen and knowledgeable volunteers. During the dormant winter months, planting begins in earnest, with each new tree being carefully caged to ward off any nibbling rabbits or deer.

So where do all the new trees come from? Many are grown from seeds and carefully tended on site in a specialist propagation unit. Here, hundreds of young plants are raised each year in greenhouses, polytunnels and shaded frames, ready to replace any losses in the grounds, and to plant up new areas. 'Wild' seeds are collected on special expeditions to their native lands – from as far afield as Japan and the USA. Closer to home, cuttings are taken from Westonbirt's own trees and cleverly grafted or layered to produce new plants.

Grass cutting is also a major operation. For nine months of the year the grass is trimmed to keep up appearances. And precision cutting at different times and to different lengths also encourages a wealth of wild flowers.

Westonbirt is a Grade 1 listed landscape, and this stunning landscape must be looked after as much as the trees. Given the potential threat from climate change and new diseases, everything possible is being done to fully appreciate the Holfords' grand Victorian plan, and ensure that we value and protect each and every plant for decades to come.

As a scientific collection, it's vital that all the plants in the arboretum are meticulously mapped, and that their origins and management are continually recorded. Westonbirt currently has about 110 champion trees – the tallest or 'fattest' of their kind in the country. Each of these important trees now bears a blue specimen label, denoting its status.

As experts delve further back into the extensive records, more and more rarities are coming to light within the vast collection – extravagant Victorian rhododendrons and exquisite trees that are struggling to survive in the wild. As well as a place of great beauty, Westonbirt is a safe haven for these rare and endangered plants and, equally importantly, a potential future gene pool. As with any great treasure, this history and growing expertise is ensuring a healthy future both for the trees and their splendid garden. Westonbirt is no longer a private pleasure ground for the few, but a much-loved and safe haven for many.